BRITAIN IN OLD PHOTOGRAPHS

SCUNTHORPE & DISTRICT

DAVID J. TAYLOR

First published 2010

The History Press
The Mill, Brimscombe Port
Stroud, Gloucestershire, GL5 2QG
www.thehistorypress.co.uk

© David J. Taylor, 2010

The right of David J. Taylor to be identified as the Author
of this work has been asserted in accordance with the
Copyrights, Designs and Patents Act 1988.

All rights reserved. No part of this book may be reprinted
or reproduced or utilised in any form or by any electronic,
mechanical or other means, now known or hereafter invented,
including photocopying and recording, or in any information
storage or retrieval system, without the permission in writing
from the Publishers.
British Library Cataloguing in Publication Data.
A catalogue record for this book is available from the British Library.

ISBN 978 0 7524 5523 5

Typesetting and origination by The History Press
Printed in Great Britain

CONTENTS

	Introduction	5
1	Village Days	7
2	Scunthorpe between 1900 and 1914	15
3	Inter-War Scunthorpe	29
4	Scunthorpe in the First and Second World Wars	39
5	Post-War Scunthorpe	49
6	Industrial Scunthorpe	57
7	Burringham, Gunness and Keadby	71
8	Burton-upon-Stather	83
9	Messingham	93
10	Normanby Hall	103
11	Winterton	115

Charging hot metal into an open-hearth furnace at Redbourn Steelworks in the 1950s.

INTRODUCTION

The history of the town of Scunthorpe has been interlinked with that of its major industry, steelmaking, since it was first established in a remote part of northern Lincolnshire in the 1860s. That this was almost entirely due to the business acumen and foresight of one man, Rowland Winn, the first Lord St Oswald, is as remarkable as the way Scunthorpe quickly developed into a sizeable industrial town. Despite this, there is a great deal more to the town's history than steelmaking, as this collection of old photographs shows.

This is the second volume to be taken from the collections of North Lincolnshire Museum. It also includes images of towns and villages surrounding the town that have traditionally formed the Scunthorpe District. They include places like Burton-upon-Stather and Winterton, which, until the second half of the nineteenth century, were larger and more important than the five villages that made up Scunthorpe. These places have long and unique histories of their own, but it is not the aim of this book to tell them. Rather it is to dip back into the past and try to gain an impression of what these communities were like from around the 1850s to about 1970.

What they show is the striking contrast between Scunthorpe's industrial and urban past, and the mainly agricultural and rural origins of the places surrounding it. Only Gunness and Keadby on the River Trent can be said to resemble industrial communities near to Scunthorpe. Hopefully readers whose links are primarily with Scunthorpe will enjoy the pictures of the villages within its orbit, and vice versa.

In the case of Scunthorpe, its growth coincides fortuitously with the development of photography, when, by the 1860s, even out of the way places were being documented by the new medium. For example, the first professional photographer working in the area, James Walsham Hall of Winterton, was taking photographs of the construction of the new ironworks by this time, and many of his home town. Old photographs are thus an excellent way of seeing how Scunthorpe evolved into a town, as well as highlighting some unique aspects of its history.

It began with the building of the ironworks, and the rapid shedding of their rural roots by Ashby, Brumby, Crosby, Frodingham and Scunthorpe. As the area's population grew, the village of Scunthorpe was the first to take on urban characteristics, becoming its main administrative and shopping centre in the 1890s. By the Edwardian period, Scunthorpe was starting to become recognisably a town, with new community buildings and modern amenities, and this was formalised in 1919 when Scunthorpe & Frodingham Urban District Council was formed from the merger of two earlier UDCs.

Between the wars, Scunthorpe's upward trajectory continued, and this was recognised by the granting of its Borough Charter on 10 October 1936. After the Second World War, the population kept growing, necessitating extensive council house building, particularly in the Ashby area. This came to a halt in the 1970s and '80s with the economic recession of that era, but since then, the town has continued to develop, but more modestly. All this expansion was in tandem with the evolution of the local steel industry, and the large-scale changes that were involved.

One particular aspect of how the town has been shaped is worth noting. This is the way greenery and open spaces have been successfully incorporated into its growth since it was recommended by the town planner Patrick Abercrombie in the 1920s. It has become so much a part of Scunthorpe's urban landscape it goes unnoticed, but it fully justifies Scunthorpe's description as 'The Industrial Garden Town'.

Transport links feature in a number of photographs here. Before the construction of the Trent, Ancholme & Grimsby Railway through the area between 1861 and 1865, roads were poor, and waterways were a means of communication, rather than a barrier to it. Packet boats plied along the Rivers Ancholme, Humber and Trent, and there were numerous small ferries connecting the villages on each side of the River Trent. The railway was another part of Rowland Winn's master plan. As well as linking the new iron-making industry with the outside world, it opened up the area in a more general way, and major social changes followed in its wake. The building of the second bridge over the River Trent at Keadby was also important, giving impetus to road improvements and motorised transport.

Old photographs record how places have altered physically, and it is fascinating to see views of familiar locations like Scunthorpe High Street a hundred years ago. They also illustrate how our daily lives have changed, and can even uncover lost worlds. The photographs in the Normanby Hall chapter, dating from the period before 1963, when it was the country seat of the Sheffield family, are good examples. They depict a world that has largely disappeared, but one that many of our recent ancestors were part of, if only as domestic servants and estate staff.

The Scunthorpe chapters in this book are arranged chronologically, beginning in the Victorian period and ending in about 1970. They therefore include images from the other four villages, even though they were still separate places until the 1930s. This was the time when they finally became physically joined together, and with the granting of its Borough Charter in 1936, the transformation of the area into a modern industrial town was complete. This remarkable feat had taken less than a hundred years. The images in the first chapter are intended to show Scunthorpe's village days in the second half of the nineteenth century, although some are slightly later in date.

All the photographs in this volume have been collected by North Lincolnshire Council's Museums Service and its Library Service over many years as a permanent record of the area, and thanks are due to the hundreds of people who have generously donated original prints or loaned copies. The images have now been digitised and can be viewed online at www.northlincs.gov.uk/imagearchive. We hope you enjoy this compilation, and that it provides an insight into the relatively recent, but eventful, history of Scunthorpe and district.

David J. Taylor, 2010

1

VILLAGE DAYS

Water Lane, Frodingham, after 1900, looking towards the level crossing over the railway line, which stood near the site of today's railway station. The second building on the left is Oswald Farm, which was owned by Mr R.I. Swaby, the landlord of the Blue Bell Hotel and a leading local figure.

St Lawrence's parish church in the snow on Boxing Day 1906. This is the oldest building in Scunthorpe, dating back to the twelfth century, and it was the mother church for the area. This picture was taken after it was restored in 1841, but before the extensions of 1913 by Sir Charles Nicholson. The church's former vicarage, constructed in 1874, was transformed into Scunthorpe Borough Museum in 1953, before becoming North Lincolnshire Museum in 1996.

Brumby Hall after 1900, when it was a tenant farm. This fine seventeenth-century manor house was extended in the eighteenth century, and is the oldest domestic dwelling in Scunthorpe. This view of the front of the Hall, flanked by two Cedar of Lebanon trees, has been unchanged for the last 400 years.

Horse-drawn wagons in Old Crosby before 1900. The one on the right contains sacks of flour from John and Alfred Bratley's mill in Brigg. Crosby was the most northerly of Scunthorpe's five original villages and was an estate village owned by the Sheffield family. It developed rapidly after the turn of the nineteenth century for workers at the new Lysaght's steelworks.

A portable steam engine on a former farm in Featherbed Lane, Crosby, at the western edge of the village, where Buckingham Street stands today.

Scunthorpe High Street looking north, c. 1890. The photograph shows a mixture of dwellings from the old village, such as Edward Dore's thatched farmhouse on the right, and newer buildings. The scene changed in 1896 with the building of new shops and a Public Hall on the corner of Manley Street opposite the Blue Bell Hotel, which can be seen on the left. All the residents have come out of their homes to have their photographs taken.

Scunthorpe windmill before it ceased operating in the early 1920s. The tower and some of its associated buildings are still standing in High Street East. It was built by Uriah Long in 1858 on the site of an earlier post mill, and he was the miller throughout its working life.

Sunday promenaders in Occupation Lane, *c.* 1905. This is now Doncaster Road, which was built in 1923 to connect the town with the second bridge at Keadby, constructed in 1916.

Looking along Scotter Road towards Frodingham Viaduct, with Brumby Wood Lane on the right. The viaduct consists of eighty-five arches, but the appearance of this impressive piece of Victorian engineering became less dramatic when it was embanked in 1912.

Repairing the roof of a thatched cottage in Frodingham around 1890. Until 1910, this dwelling stood at the corner of Oswald Road and Station Road, then known as Water Lane.

Labourers and some Ashby children near the Screeds on the north side of Ashby High Street, c. 1907. The tall chimney of a traction engine can be seen in the background.

Old Brumby Street was the main street of the village of Brumby. It was still very rural in this view taken from Ashby Road at around the turn of the last century.

This sentimental old postcard of Brumby shows one of the footpaths that linked the five villages together. Some parts of them have been paved and can still be walked.

The scene in Ashby High Street near the junction with present-day Collum Avenue, *c.* 1900. James Kendall's post office, with a postman outside, and the entrance to Middleton's Yard are on the right. Many of the buildings date from before 1850, and this part of the High Street from Bottesford Road to Grange Lane South was the old village street.

Scunthorpe High Street decorated for Queen Victoria's Diamond Jubilee in 1897. On the left is the Blue Bell Hotel, which dated from the second half of the eighteenth century. It was greatly extended after 1864 into a forty-two bedroom hotel by its long-standing proprietor, Robert Ingham Swaby (1832-1915), including new stables along Manley Street. During Scunthorpe's village days and after, it was the main centre of social activity in the area, and the meeting place of many public bodies, including early trade unions.

2

SCUNTHORPE BETWEEN 1900 AND 1914

Scunthorpe Divisional Police Force taken outside the former courthouse building on Station Road after 1900.

One of Scunthorpe's most famous landmarks, the parish church of St John the Evangelist at the east end of the High Street, is depicted in this postcard taken in 1912. It was built in 1891 as a gift to the town by Rowland Winn, the first Lord St Oswald, and is now part of 20-21 Visual Arts Centre.

Inside St John's, looking across richly-carved choir stalls towards the west end of the church before the First World War.

Bell's Supply Stores at 62 High Street, at the junction of Market Hill and High Street, c. 1905. These prominently situated premises opposite the bus station were occupied a few years later by Melia's grocers shop. The aprons of the staff have been freshly starched for the occasion.

Alfred Read's confectionary stall in the new Market Hall opened by Scunthorpe Urban District Council in 1906. He also had a shop at 146 Scunthorpe High Street.

These youngsters are using the High Street as an impromptu paddling pool after flooding on 16 August 1909. The view is looking north from Cole Street at Wells Street, with the Trinity Wesleyan Church on the right, and behind it, the Lord Roberts Hotel.

Another photograph of flooding in the High Street taken on the same day. This is looking east towards Cole Street and Wells Street with the site of Barclay's Bank, also built in 1909, on the right.

A studio portrait of Henry Brace Parkhouse (1859-1939), taken after 1900. He was a steel pioneer, a Scunthorpe Urban District Councillor, and he also owned Parkhouse's cycle and furniture shop at 58 High Street, which can be seen on the left of the previous photograph. As well as bicycles, his shop also sold mangles, washers, hand and treadle sewing machines, bedsteads, spring and wool mattresses, wool and feather beds, children's cots and other household requisites.

The Blue Bell Hotel decorated for the Coronation of George V in 1911. In advertisements it was described as a 'Family, commercial and posting house', and the hotel were agents to 'The Great Central Railway for the delivery of goods and parcels'. It was demolished in 1970 when the shopping precinct was built.

Above left: Burton-on-Trent brewer Ind Coope & Co. Ltd's off-license at 50 Scunthorpe High Street in 1912, opposite the Blue Bell Hotel. As well as 'Fine sparkling ales and extra stout', they also sold 'Wines and spirits of the best quality, single bottles at wholesale prices'.

Above right: Price's 6½d Bazaar at 87 High Street, near Belgrave Square, at around the turn of the twentieth century. The proprietor, John Henry Price, is standing in the doorway, and Jessie, his eldest daughter, is in the pram pushed by the family maid. The shop is selling household goods for 6½d or less ranging from baskets, brushes, carpet beaters and cooking pots to stools and shovels. The concept of cheap bazaars originated in America.

Left: Mary Blanchard outside her tobacconist's shop at 121 High Street, between Belgrave Square and Ravendale Street, *c.* 1905.

A church parade consisting of Territorial Army soldiers of the Lincolnshire Yeomanry, No. 3 Scunthorpe Troop, marching down High Street on 25 April 1909. At the head of the troop are Mr W. Woodley and Mr J. Fowler, and the single-storey building next to Cemetery Road, now Frances Street, was the 'wooden studio' of local photographer Arthur Henry Singleton.

Immaculately polished hand pumps, gas lights and decorated stained glass behind the bar of the Oswald Hotel in around 1910. The 'Oswald' has been open for customers in the High Street since 1896, and is now known as Harry Charlesworths.

Station Road, now High Street East, c. 1908. Scunthorpe, Frodingham & District Working Men's Constitutional Club is on the left (opened in 1897), next door to the first library, opened seven years later. Scunthorpe Museum began here in a room in the basement in 1909. In the centre is Herbert Spilman's, stone, marble and granite mason's yard.

Stonemasons at Spilman's yard in Station Road, demonstrating a large masonry saw in 1905. The business was started here by William Spilman in 1883, before his son, Herbert William Spilman, took over in 1900. In advertisements they offered 'All kinds of monumental work. Old stones cleaned and additional inscriptions cut. Wreathes a speciality.'

Station Road, now High Street East, after 1910, when it was the main thoroughfare leading to the iron and steel works. In the background is Scunthorpe courthouse and police station, erected in 1894, and on the extreme right is Scunthorpe windmill. The first poster is advertising Kirkpatrick's drapers shop in Wells Street, and everyone seems aware of the camera man, apart from the painter and decorator working on the left.

Pupils from Scunthorpe Church of England School photographed in Gurnell Street from Wells Street, *c.* 1910. The school buildings, opened in 1895, can be seen at the end of the street.

Show horses at Scunthorpe Agricultural Show on 7 July 1909. This was on Doncaster Road on the site of the 'Old Showground', Scunthorpe United FC's former stadium until they moved to Glanford Park in 1988.

Rowland Road before 1910, with Frodingham School the first building on the left (built in 1867), next door to Frodingham Parish Church Institute, opened in 1905. This was built some distance from St Lawrence's parish church for the benefit of people living in New Frodingham.

Terrace houses complete with small front gardens and iron railings in Mill Road, Ashby, *c.* 1908. This is now the upper part of Ashby High Street with Victoria Road on the right, but at this time it was named after Ashby Windmill. This was a wooden post mill, which stood on Ashby Road near Ashby Turn until around 1900.

Staff members and a delivery wagon outside Charles Gant's grocers and drapers shop in Ashby High Street, *c.* 1906. This long-standing business stood opposite the Crown Hotel, and in 1931 specialised in 'tea, coffee and best quality bacon and ham'.

Left: Frederick Keal's fish and chip shop on Ashby High Street. He is advertising deliveries of fresh fish on Wednesdays and Saturdays, which would have arrived by train from Grimsby.

Below: The Revd A.V. Chapman, the vicar of St Paul's Church, Ashby, with members of his congregation after spring cleaning the church. This was the iron 'Tin Tabernacle' erected in 1899, which preceded the present church opened in 1925.

Looking down Ashby High Street with the second and third Ashby Wesleyan Methodist chapels on the left, opened in 1871 and 1907 respectively. The whitewashed building at the corner of Stockshill Road was a wheelwright and joiner's shop.

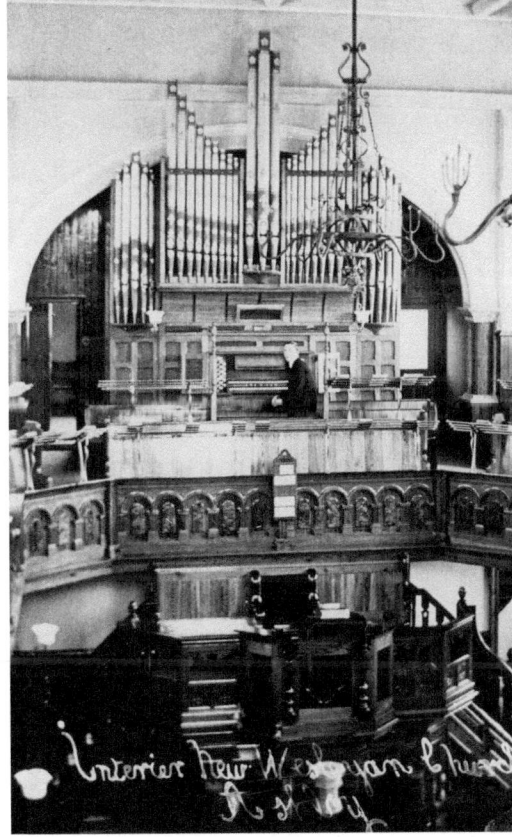

The interior of Ashby Wesleyan Chapel after it opened on 10 July 1907, with Harry Parker Watson at the organ. The stained-glass windows in the chapel were installed after the First World War to commemorate twenty-two members of the congregation who lost their lives in the conflict. The entire building thus became a fitting memorial to them.

Ashby Constitutional Club, decorated for the Coronation of George V in 1911. Built in 1896, it stood on the south side of Ashby High Street opposite Ashby Junior School. Its premises are now at the north end of Everest Road.

A group of house builders in Ashby. They were a common sight in the town, as it grew rapidly alongside the burgeoning steel industry.

3

INTER-WAR SCUNTHORPE

Scunthorpe Hospital Carnival parade in the High Street in the 1920s, with Miss Gant driving the decorated motorcar. It is *en route* from St John's Church to the Co-operative showground in Brumby Wood Lane, where the main carnival day event was held. The carnival began in 1923, and soon became one of the highlights of the town's social calendar between the wars. It was a way of raising money for the local hospital, and consisted of a week of activities culminating in a spectacular programme of entertainment on Carnival Day. This included band performances, boxing, dancing, fireworks, ox-roasts, sideshows and the famous North Lincolnshire 'flitch' trial. The latter was a light-hearted competition based on the ancient Dunmow flitch trials, designed to find the happiest married couple in the district!

Scunthorpe High Street in the early 1920s, close to the junction with Cemetery Road, now Frances Street. The fashionable iron veranda on the right overhung a draper's, a fruit shop, a house furnisher, an ironmonger's and a shoe shop.

One of Tommy Fisher's famous window displays at his butcher's shop at 72 High Street, between Market Hill and Wells Street.

The High Street looking east in 1936, with F.W. Woolworth's 3d and 6d stores on the left opposite Marks and Spencer's bazaar. The decorations were for the town's Borough Charter celebrations, which was officially granted on 10 October of that year after four days of celebrations. The van parked on the right belonged to the London & North Eastern Railway.

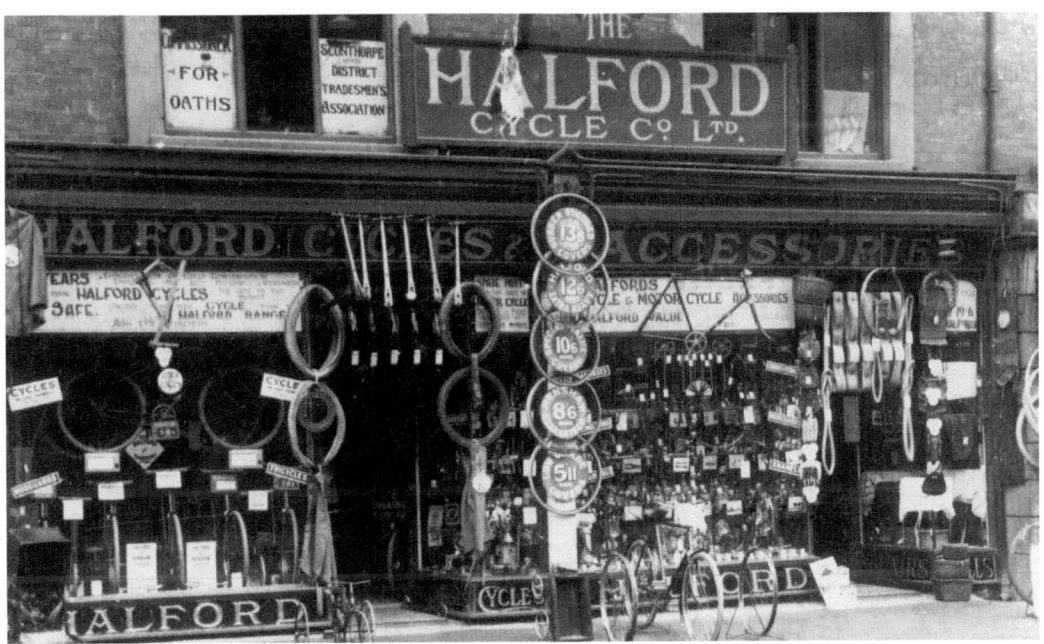

Halford's cycle shop at 94 High Street after 1926. The company was formed as a local hardware store by Mr F.W. Rushbrooke in Birmingham in 1892. By 1910, they had over 100 branches throughout the country.

A floodlit view of Scunthorpe Public Baths on the evening of 24 March 1932, after the official opening earlier in the day. The new public baths were Scunthorpe & Frodingham Urban District Council's most ambitious building project, designed by Mr W. Fararr, the Council's engineer and surveyor. Its facilities consisted of two swimming pools, sixteen slipper baths, a laundry and Club rooms in the basement. Functions were held from the start, when the Adult Baths, or 'big baths', were boarded over with a polished maple floor in the winter months. This was partly a way of saving money by not heating the pool. The dance floor could accommodate 680 people.

The Globe cinema on Ashby High Street in 1928. It was built by Mr W.H. Webster in 1926, and its plain frontage is that of a single-storey village picture house. When sound was introduced in 1929, it was described as 'The prettiest cinema in the district', of which there were seven in Scunthorpe alone. It was renamed the Roxy in 1953, but closed on 27 February 1962, following a projection room fire. The building still survives, and part of it is now a public house called the Malt Shovel.

A decorated float made by Heald's grocer's shop in the Scunthorpe Hospital Carnival parade of 1927.

Sir Berkeley Sheffield of Normanby Hall is standing on the left of this photograph at the official opening of Sheffield Park on 26 May 1926. He gave 11 acres of land to the north of Ferry Road for Scunthorpe's first public park, which included ornamental gardens, tennis courts, bowling greens and a bandstand.

The unveiling and dedication ceremony of Ashby War Memorial on 31 May 1925 by Sir Berkeley Sheffield, following a parade along Ashby High Street. It consists of a Celtic cross mounted on a marble column, and this is its original site opposite Ashby Turn. It was moved to its present location outside St Paul's Church in 1963.

The foundation laying ceremony of Scunthorpe War Memorial Hospital on 13 October 1927. Lord Buckland of Bwelch laid the foundation stone using a silver trowel, and a room was named after him when the hospital opened on 29 December 1929. The new hospital was a memorial to servicemen from the area who lost their lives in the First World War, and was the beginning of today's General Hospital.

HRH Prince George, the Duke of Kent, cutting the ribbon to open the new section of the Doncaster to Grimsby trunk road through Scunthorpe on 26 October 1933. This is better known today as Kingsway and Queensway, and Prince George (the fourth son of King George V), was the first member of the Royal family to visit Scunthorpe.

The staff of Scunthorpe Co-operative Society's No. 2 branch outside the shop in the lower part of Ashby High Street after the First World War. It was opened on 10 October 1896 by Mr G. Reed, the president of the Society for that year, after complaints from Ashby members that their nearest branch was in Scunthorpe. At one time, the Co-op was the biggest retailer in Scunthorpe.

Dale's butcher's shop at the corner of Ashby High Street and Queen Street.

Frederick Drayton with his Scunthorpe & District Motors' omnibus in the 1930s. He operated the Ashby to Scunthorpe route as well as running to Appleby.

A single-deck Red Progressive omnibus with crew – including Mr J.A. 'Roundy' Foster – leaning out of the cab window. This early Scunthorpe company was bought out by Enterprise & Silver Dawn Motors Ltd in 1925.

The award ceremony at Scunthorpe Chrysanthemum Show on 15 November 1938. The cup for the most points in the open section is being presented to Mrs J. Buckle of The Nurseries, Gunness. In the background are some of the prize-winning blooms.

The Scunthorpe United team during the 1922/3 season, in their Midland League days at the Old Showground on Doncaster Road. The gas holders were part of the local council's gasworks, on site of the former Baths Hall, and the 'Knuts' was United's first nickname.

4

SCUNTHORPE IN THE FIRST AND SECOND WORLD WARS

Erecting an Anderson shelter at the start of the Second World War, in the garden of 75 Exeter Road, at the corner of Exeter Road and Church Lane. In front of the shelter are, from left to right, Amy Smith, with her neighbours Esther Grocock, Hazel Grocock and Donald Grocock. Behind are Amy's husband and son.

A family with two of its members in uniform. This is the Robinson family of 28 Manley Street, taken by John Moon, who had studios in Scunthorpe and Brigg. Arthur Robinson served as an Able-Bodied Seaman on board the HMS *Boyne*, and his brother, Walter, was a Private in the 6th Battalion of the Lincolnshire Regiment. Both survived the First World War.

Empire Day at Ashby Infants School during the First World War. This annual event was held to promote the British Empire on the anniversary of Queen Victoria's birthday. During the war, the children raised money to send comforts to the troops fighting at the front. The four in the centre are dressed to represent the four countries of the United Kingdom with Britannia at the front. The school's headmistress, Miss Drake, is standing on the left of the photograph.

Arthur 'Harry' Singleton (on the left) was Scunthorpe's leading photographer in the first quarter of the last century. During the First World War he served in Palestine as a photographer with the 40th Wing of the Royal Flying Corps, but this may have led to his untimely death in 1927, aged 47.

Left: One brave soldier who did not return home was William Aubrey Horne of 18 Smith Street. He was a private in the 8th Battalion of the Lincolnshire Regiment, but was killed on 26 September 1915 at the Battle of Loos.

Below: Cyril 'Sid' Allen DCM, on a Norton motorcycle in Scunthorpe. He was a gunner in the Tank Corps and was awarded the Distinguished Conduct Medal, second only to the Victoria Cross, for 'conspicuous bravery and devotion to duty'. He unfortunately lost his life during the Battle of Cambrai, on 20 November 1917.

A crowd dressed in their best clothes on Frodingham Road in 1919 watch the Crosby peace celebrations for the signing of the Treaty of Versailles, which formally ended the First World War.

The welcome home reception at Normanby Hall in 1919, for servicemen returning from the First World War.

A First World War tank nicknamed 'Egbert' outside the east end of St John's Church in around 1925. This was given to the town after the conflict in recognition of the money raised in War Bonds and Saving Certificates. In late 1917, they were taken round the country as publicity tools to raise money for the war effort, and became known as 'tank banks'. It is not known what eventually happened to Egbert.

Royal Navy destroyer, HMS *Vanity*, taken during the Second World War. She was adopted by Scunthorpe during 'Warship Week' in December 1941, and in October 1943, officers from the ship visited the town. Commissioned in 1918, she was armed with four 4ins guns and six torpedo tubes, and survived the conflict, only to be scrapped in 1947.

HM King George VI and Queen Elizabeth at Lysaght's Steelworks, during their morale-raising visit to Scunthorpe on 1 August 1940, when they were also given a tour of Appleby-Frodingham Steelworks. King George VI is wearing the uniform of a Field Marshal.

A Civil Defence gas attack and gas mask demonstration in Scunthorpe High Street, opposite Ravendale Street.

A wrecked German Heinkel bomber in transit through Scunthorpe, parked in Doncaster Road on 27 March 1941, with Police Sergeant Francis in the foreground. Six of these bombers were shot down in the area between late February and early November 1941.

The 4th Lindsey Battalion of the Home Guard, taken during the war behind Brumby Hall in Scunthorpe.

These large steel structures, seen here in 1943, were made by the Scunthorpe firm of Orthostyle Ltd as part of the D-Day 'Pipe line under the ocean' (PLUTO) project.

The Victory in Europe (VE) Day street party in Smith Street on 8 May 1945.

Celebrations on Victory over Japan (VJ) Day in Princess Street on 15 August 1945. Princess Street was a narrow terrace of houses off Crosby Road to the north of Scunthorpe High Street, renowned for its street parties.

Remains of the former Empire Theatre at the corner of Manley Street and High Street in 1948. It was built as a Public Hall in 1896, but later became a theatre, and showed silent films between 1910 and 1930. It was burnt out in a fire in 1942, when in use as an Armed Forces' canteen.

5
POST-WAR SCUNTHORPE

Celebrating the Coronation of HM Queen Elizabeth II at Priory Lane Infants School on 2 June 1953. Each child received a commemorative cup, saucer and plate, and a large slice of fruitcake!

Britannia Corner in around 1955, when cycling was still a popular way of getting to work. In the background on Frodingham Road is the tower and spire of the original Centenary Methodist Chapel, opened in 1908.

This is the 'west end' of Scunthorpe High Street in 1964, when there were a number of different Scunthorpe Co-operative Society shops located there. On the left is their main Central Emporium (a department store), which was extended in 1967 and re-named Ashton House. It had an early digital-type clock on the front, which sets the time of the photograph as 2.55 p.m. on Tuesday 11 August.

The High Street in the mid-1950s, looking towards Britannia Corner and Scunthorpe Congregational Church at the end of Oswald Road, built in 1912.

Scunthorpe's first bus station on a rainy day in the late 1960s, before demolition in 1968. It was built in 1929 by the Enterprise & Silver Dawn bus company.

Scunthorpe & District War Memorial on Oswald Road, outside the entrance to Scunthorpe Museum & Art Gallery. The date is 1955 or after, because it was relocated here from Doncaster Road in that year. The Bridge Hotel is in the background, also constructed by Hull Brewery in 1955 in a semi-circular shape to match the General Post Office on the other side of the road. The roundabout, which once stood at the junction of Church Lane, Oswald Road and Station Road, can also be seen.

The annual Scunthorpe Museum Art Group outdoor exhibition in Vicarage Gardens, c. 1970. This popular August bank holiday event continues to be held to this day.

Herbert Kirman's stall at a Scunthorpe Agricultural Show, Trade & Industrial Exhibition and Athletics Meeting in around 1950, at the 'Showground Brumby Wood Lane', now Quibell Park. He ran a large ironmonger's shop on Market Hill, boasting 'the most varied stock in the district'.

The formal opening of the model traffic area on Laneham Street by HM Queen Elizabeth II, during her official visit to Scunthorpe on 27 June 1958. It was used to teach children cycling proficiency until 1974, but the site is now occupied by the Park Square office complex. HRH Prince Phillip, the Duke of Edinburgh, is on the right.

Kingsway Gardens in around 1960, after the completion of the formal gardens, including a lily pond in the centre. Doncaster Road is on the right and Keadby Power Station in the background. These gardens are part of a network of linked open spaces running along the western escarpment of the town.

Festival gardens on Ashby Road were opened by General Sir Richard Gale in 1951 and were the first stage in the development of Central Park. They were named after the Festival of Britain held in that year, and the centrepiece was this concrete shelter known as the 'rotunda', erected by local firm Hydroprest Ltd.

Scunthorpe's new Civic Centre building and Council Chamber after opening in 1963. It was designed by C.B. Pearson and Partners of Lancaster, and re-named Pittwood House in 1996. This view was taken from Queens Gardens South, which was named after the Coronation of HM Queen Elizabeth II in 1953. She planted a beech tree here near Ashby Road during her visit to Scunthorpe in 1958.

The scene at Appleby-Frodingham works gala on 3 June 1967, in the grounds of Brumby Hall Sports Club.

British Iron & Steel Federation houses in East Common Lane, c. 1960. Three hundred and fifty of these prefabricated, semi-detached 'steel houses' were built throughout Scunthorpe in 1948 to help ease the chronic post-war housing shortage. They were designed to last sixty years but are all still standing today, and are immediately recognisable by the steel cladding on their upper floors.

The new east grandstand at Scunthorpe United FC's Old Showground in 1958, now the site of Sainsbury's supermarket. Constructed and erected by the United Steel Structural Company, it was the first cantilever stand in the country, with a capacity of 2,351. This type of stand was designed to give spectators an uninterrupted view of events unfolding on the pitch.

6

INDUSTRIAL SCUNTHORPE

Ironstone miners, called 'sanders', working in a local mine in the early part of the last century. Their job was to remove the topsoil covering the ironstone, which often involved barrowing it across plank runways standing high above the ground.

'Chuckers' digging out ironstone and loading it into railway wagons at Yarborough Mine. Inspectors like the one on the right were employed by the various early ironworks companies to keep a close eye on the quality of their ore. The height of some of the runways used by the sanders can be seen in the background.

Opposite above: A German 'dredger' type excavator working in Ashby Mine in April 1910. Mechanical excavators started to be used in Scunthorpe in ironstone mines around this time, although hand working continued until the 1930s.

Opposite below: Winterton Road Remine ironstone mine in Scunthorpe on 22 October 1956, with a steam shovel loading railway wagons.

Construction work at Frodingham Ironworks on 29 June 1903. The blast furnaces are on the right, opposite the Station Hotel, and beyond them are St John's Church and Scunthorpe windmill.

Appleby Ironworks, c. 1891. They were the most easterly situated of Scunthorpe's six original works, first producing iron in 1876. Frodingham Iron & Steel Company bought them out in 1912 and they became known as 'North Ironworks'. These blast furnaces finally ceased operating in 1954.

Blast furnacemen at North Lincoln Ironworks around the turn of the last century.

Pig casters at Lysaght's Steelworks after it opened in 1912. The leather aprons in front of them were worn for protection from molten iron.

Working on the new coke ovens at Redbourn Ironworks on 16 May 1919, during the redevelopment project that turned it from a small ironworks into a modern, integrated plant.

A rolling mill under construction during the Redbourn redevelopment on 18 April 1919.

Female workers at Appleby-Frodingham Plate Mills in 1950, including Celia Bones from Broughton. During both world wars, women took over jobs in the steel industry left by men serving in the Armed Forces. Some, like these ladies, stayed on after the second conflict.

Santon Mining Company opened Scunthorpe's first underground ironstone mine in 1938. Here miners are working at the ironstone face on 1 August 1942. Jack Bickerdike is about to introduce a cartridge of gelignite into a hole, with Tommy Busby standing by with a charging stick and clay-stemming cartridge.

Frodingham Iron & Steel Company 0-6-0 saddle tank locomotive No. 12, c. 1920. It was made by Andrew Barclay & Sons Co. of Kilmarnock in 1905, but was sold to Eccles Slag in 1945.

Merchant vessel *Elizabeth Lysaght* moored at Flixborough Wharf on the River Trent. The wharf was built in 1938 by Lysaght's Steelworks to ship steel to their works in Newport in South Wales, and a short railway line connected it to their Normanby Park works.

Erecting the starkly modern spire of the Church of the Holy Spirit on Willoughby Road in August 1963. It was one of many steel structural projects undertaken in the town, and throughout the world, by the United Steel Structural Company, in this case for the architect Derek Brown. Technically known as a 'welded box section tripod', the tower weighs 16 tons and rises to a height of 120ft.

United Steel Structural Company also constructed the roof of the new Civic Centre Council Chamber on Ashby Road, weighing 20 tons. It is seen here on 23 June 1963.

Emmanuel Airstrip, built by United Steel Companies in 1959, on land east of Ashby Ville alongside the A18 Scunthorpe to Brigg road. It was used by private aeroplanes visiting their works, and was also the base for three small company aircraft. It ceased operating when the new Anchor steelmaking project began to be built on the site in 1969. The name came from a group of nearby houses.

Workers at the former Frodingham Chemical Works on Brigg Road, taken on 19 September 1906 amongst the debris of the fire which destroyed the factory two days earlier.

Staff outside the offices of Scunthorpe Urban District Council's Gas Department in Belgrave Square. By 1914, they were supplying gas to businesses and homes throughout the area, initially from the former gas works on the site of the Baths Hall on Doncaster Road and after 1923 from Dawes Lane.

Borough of Scunthorpe Gas Department float in the Hospital Carnival parade of 1938, standing in High Street East. The 'chef' is Henry Brewer.

Arthur Henry Singleton, a local photographer, is riding this early motorcycle along Brumby Wood Lane, *c.* 1903. It was made by Johnson Cycles, who manufactured bicycles from 1890 and motorcycles from 1901 at Trafford Street, and then at their Beeston Cycle and Motor Works in Home Street. The passenger is Arthur's mother, Elizabeth.

A delivery van belonging to Radiance Confectionery, founded by Philip Jackson in 1919. They made toffee and sweets in Gilliatt Street and Cole Street, before moving to Doncaster in the mid-1920s, where there was a flourishing sweet manufacturing industry.

A Brumpton's brewery delivery wagon outside Scunthorpe Cemetery in around 1913. It belonged to William T. Brumpton, who had a botanical brewery at 24 West Street, making dandelion and burdock, ginger beer, mineral waters and sarsaparilla. They were taken over by Riley's Potato Crisps in 1963, by which time their factory was at 32 Normanby Road.

Loading tins of Riley's crisps outside their first factory in Allanby Street in 1956. Riley's Potato Crisps was started by Alfred 'Biff' Riley and his brother Dennis at their father's fish and chip shop in West Street in 1947. By the end of the 1970s, Riley's had become the fifth largest crisp manufacturer in the country. This retail van salesman is carrying ten tins of crisps. The record was twelve!

These lady operatives are picking out burnt crisps amongst the freshly fried ones coming out of the cooker at Riley's second factory at Colin Road in the mid-1960s. The company moved there in 1960, and Ken Boyd is the supervisor.

These ladies are packing boxes by hand at the Riley's factory in Colin Road in the mid-1960s.

7

BURRINGHAM, GUNNESS AND KEADBY

Sailing barges on the Stainforth & Keadby Canal waiting to enter Keadby Lock, and into the River Trent. Behind the railway wagons is Keadby Loco, which was the main railway depot in the Scunthorpe area until 1932. The Stainforth & Keadby Canal was opened in 1802 to link the River Trent with the Don Navigation, allowing goods from the Humber to reach Sheffield and South Yorkshire more easily.

Burringham High Street looking north in 1905. Signalman John William Horner is in the centre in railway uniform, with his son Albert. Behind them is coal merchant Herbert Jaques, with one foot on his dray. The new terraced housing on the left contrasts with the thatched cottage on the right, which is badly in need of repair.

Two shops owned by John Tuton in Burringham High Street, *c.* 1905. On the left is the village post office, and next door, his grocer's and draper's shop. He is standing with his wife in the doorway.

This view of the High Street in 1915 shows the post office owned by John Tock after 1911 on the left, with Burringham Primitive Methodist Chapel, built in 1836, on the opposite side of the road.

The attractive parish church of St John the Baptist in Burringham was built mainly in red brick by the renowned Victorian architect Samuel Sanders Teulon between 1856 and 1857. It became redundant in 1982, and is now looked after by the Churches Conservation Trust.

Mrs Jewitt outside her cottage in Burringham High Street. The cottage was demolished in the early 1930s.

Burringham Ferry looking towards the landing stage on the opposite bank of the River Trent, near the Dolphin Hotel at Althorpe. On the left is the parish church of St Oswald, built in 1483.

Herbert Jaques was a coal merchant and later a farmer in Burringham, and is seen here on the right with his family around the time of the First World War.

Burringham plough jags, taken by photographer Arthur Singleton outside his studio in Scunthorpe High Street before 1920. They were an unusual two-horse team, who were one of the last to cease performing in the area in 1939.

The Jolly Sailor public house in Gunness in the 1950s, advertising Hewitt's Ales of Grimsby. It was built by Sergeant's Brewery of Brigg, who were bought out by Hewitt's in 1945.

The barge Irby, loaded with slag, at Gunness Wharf in 1939, with Keadby Bridge to the south.

The southern end of Station Road, Gunness, in the 1920s.

An Edwardian postcard of St Barnabas' Church. In 1952, it was replaced by the present church on Station Road, which now serves Burringham as well as Gunness.

A display mounted in Scunthorpe by Joseph Buckle in 1949. He was a local florist with nurseries on Gunness Straight, and also in Scunthorpe on Scotter Road near Quibell Park.

The first railway bridge over the River Trent at Keadby, taken from the west bank looking towards Gunness. It was a swing bridge, and was officially opened in 1865 as part of the Trent Ancholme & Grimsby Railway, which linked Keadby with Barnetby through the new Frodingham ironstone district.

A view taken from Keadby on the west bank of the River Trent of the King George V combined rail and road bridge, opened in 1916. It replaced the older bridge, which was demolished in 1920, although it can still be seen to the south of this photograph. It is a Scherzer Rolling Lift Bridge, built by William Arrol & Son of Glasgow, and is the longest of its type in the country.

The heavy steel girderwork of Keadby Bridge stands out in this photograph, taken on the roadway side of the bridge, *c.* 1930.

A busy day on the River Trent at the point where it is joined at Keadby by the Stainforth & Keadby Canal.

Shops, including Dunstan's grocers shop and the Friendship Hotel, alongside the towpath on the Stainforth & Keadby near Keadby Lock, *c.* 1910. The landlord of the Friendship Hotel at this time was Robert Oldfield.

The caption to this postcard rather optimistically describes this scene showing a row of shops next to the South Yorkshire Hotel as 'Market Place Keadby'. They include Bramhill's Boot Stores, and the railway track led to a coal chute for railway wagons on the River Trent.

Trentside, to the north of Keadby, *c.* 1937. On the right is the Wesleyan Methodist Chapel, built in 1861.

Althorpe & Keadby railway station in the 1950s, looking towards Keadby Bridge. In 1916 it replaced two stations; one on each side of the original railway bridge. They were known as 'Keadby & Althorpe' and 'Gunness & Burringham'.

A Keadby Primitive Methodist Chapel charabanc outing in 1921.

8

BURTON-UPON-STATHER

Looking down at Burton Stather from the top of Stather Road. 'Stather' is a Danish word meaning landing place, and a small hamlet grew up here close to the Ferryboat Inn and the ferry across the River Trent to Garthorpe.

Burton-upon-Stather High Street around 1900, with the Primitive Methodist chapel, built in 1868, on the right.

View of the High Street in the opposite direction, taken from the Sheffield Arms public house in around 1930. Wilfred Pugsley's Dugout Bus Company ran a regular service from Burton to Scunthorpe at this time.

Looking north along the High Street after the First World War. James Sutton's saddler and harness makers shop is on the right, opposite Alderson Brown's grocers shop and the village post office.

The Sheffield Arms public house. This picture was taken after 1930, the date it was bought from the Sheffield family by W.M. Darley's Brewery of Thorne. It was built in 1687 as the Black Bull, before it was purchased and rebuilt by the Sheffields, who then re-named it.

Cyril Saunby's general store at the corner of the High Street and Stather Road in the 1930s. The lychgate to St Andrew's Church, built in 1910, is just visible on the right.

This view of the High Street is looking south, after 1915. The village stands on the brow of the Cliff overlooking the River Trent, and was once a small market town.

St Andrew's parish church dates from the twelfth century, but it is mainly Early English in style. It was restored in 1865 and 1889, and contains monuments to the Sheffield family. In 1777 it was damaged by an explosion on board a ship in the River Trent.

Inside the church, looking towards the chancel. The unusual arch decorated with chevron ornament on the left of the photograph is one of three dating from the Norman period, when the church was first built.

The dedication ceremony of the new vestry on 31 July 1938, by the Dean of Lincoln.

The terrace houses in this photograph were known as 'Old Row', and were built for workers in two brick yards situated side-by-side, just south of the Stather. John Franks & Sons was working them by the 1920s, but one had earlier been the Normanby Estate brick yard.

Stather Hill from 'Old Row' in 1913.

The *Atlanta* moored at the pier at Burton-upon-Stather. She was one of the packet boats owned by the Gainsborough United Steam Packet Co. Ltd that worked from Gainsborough to Hull. The services started in the early years of the nineteenth century, and went on into the 1930s. They typically left Gainsborough at 6 a.m., returning at 2 p.m.

The crew of a sailing barge at the Stather enjoying a cooked meal between the wars.

A picnic party from St John's Church Women's Guild in Scunthorpe at Burton Hills, *c.* 1908. At this time it was the area's local beauty spot.

This post mill stood on the approach to Burton from Normanby, and was still working when this photograph was taken after the turn of the last century. It may have been built in the 1730s and is thought to have been demolished in the 1930s, when it was owned by the Drury family.

Humber Road Car Services motorcoach FW3800 waiting outside the Blue Bell Hotel in Scunthorpe with a service to Burton in the 1930s. Mr Cuthbert Rowbottom is about to board the bus. Several operators north of Scunthorpe merged to form this company to stave off takeover by the Enterprise & Silver Dawn company in Scunthorpe, including Walter Pugsley's in Burton.

The Avenue, looking west in the snow in around 1970, with the original beech trees – planted in the nineteenth century – on either side of the road.

9

MESSINGHAM

Messingham High Street looking north after 1900. Standing in the road is the 'Cross tree', which replaced an earlier one in 1878, but was removed in the 1920s as motor traffic increased. Next to it is the Green Tree public house, whose name is derived from it.

Looking south along the High Street in Edwardian days. The building second from the end of the row of buildings on the left is the Horn Inn, which was converted into a coaching inn during the late eighteenth century. Beyond is a large barn, which was demolished in the 1960s.

Modwen House is on the left of this view of the junction with Well Street on the south side of the High Street in around 1925.

Arthur Berry's tailors and drapers shop in Messingham High Street before 1913. He was also a newsagent, and is advertising 'pictorial post cards' in his shop window, at a time when postcards were avidly collected.

Standing outside his village post office and grocer's shop in Messingham High Street is Aaron Bristow with members of his family. This photograph was taken around 1910 and, like Arthur Berry's shop, local postcards are also displayed in his shop window.

Left: Messingham War Memorial is situated on a prominent site to the north of the village, near the junction of High Street and Northfield Road. It was unveiled on 26 September 1920, and consists of a simple cross decorated with a crown mounted on a pedestal. It commemorates all the men from the village who lost their lives in the two world wars, and one from a later conflict in Bosnia.

Below: Messingham Hall or 'High Hall' on Northfield Road. It may have replaced an earlier Hall called Low Hall in the late eighteenth century, and was owned by John Henry Price in the 1920s.

Looking down Church Street from the High Street at the beginning of the last century. The first building on the right is the schoolroom to Messingham Wesleyan Methodist Chapel, built in 1869, with the chapel itself next door opened in 1821. This was the second Wesleyan Mehodist chapel in the village.

Butterwick Road, *c.* 1910. This picture was taken by Grayson Clarke, a local photographer who worked in Scotter and then Brigg from around 1905 to the early 1930s. He liked to fill his views with people, presumably so they would buy copies from him!

Holy Trinity parish church. Although dating from the thirteenth century, all of the exterior apart from the tower was rebuilt for the then vicar of Messingham, Dr Henry Vincent Bayley, between 1817 and 1818. Dr Bayley was also the Sub-Dean of Lincoln and Archbishop of Stow, and a noted antiquarian and scholar. He decorated his church with fragments of stained glass and other monuments from churches in Lincolnshire and further afield, and was perhaps unfairly accused of 'robbing' them.

The interior of Holy Trinity Church, showing arches and columns from the original church, built in the Early English style.

A 1960s view looking north towards Messingham High Street from Scotter Road, with Brigg Road on the right. One of Messingham's landmarks, a building with a complicated history known as 'Trentholme', is just out of view on the left opposite the junction. The main part was built in 1875, but it is best known for its connection with the Dawes family, who made the first iron in Scunthorpe. In the 1880s, it was the home of Joshua Dawes, the son of William Henry Dawes, who managed the Trent Ironworks. From a prospect tower he could view his ironworks in Scunthorpe, five miles away.

The signpost at the junction of Messingham High Street and Brigg Road in 1926. The cottage in the background on Brigg Road is one of the oldest buildings in the village, dating from around 1700.

New bungalows on Eastfield Road in the 1960s. Messingham has grown considerably since the Second World War, with most of the development taking place on the north side of the High Street.

Farmer Joseph Hair with his family outside Briggate Farm, off Brigg Road, *c.* 1912. They are, from left to right: Edgar, Joseph, Eleanor, Leonard and Ronald Hair, Charles Jackson (Joseph's father-in-law) and George Hair.

A Royal Mail horse and trap at Messingham post office before the First World War. The postman is Mr Fenton.

Goodson & Wright's omnibus in Messingham before 1928. They were one of the first local companies to be taken over by the Enterprise & Silver Dawn company in Scunthorpe, who became the biggest in the area running services as far as Lincoln. They were themselves taken over by the Lincolnshire Road Car company in 1950.

A Combined Fire Services demonstration in Messingham in 1942. These are members of the women's section of the National Fire Service.

10

NORMANBY HALL

Normanby Hall has been the home of the Sheffield family since the late sixteenth century. These photographs show it before it was leased to Scunthorpe Borough Council, now North Lincolnshire Council, in 1963. This is the Hall from the south drive around the time of the First World War. It was originally part of the main road between Scunthorpe and Burton-upon-Stather, but it was converted into a drive when the present Hall was constructed by Sir Robert Smirke between 1825 and 1830.

The Hall in 1876, decorated for the celebrations at Normanby for the birth of Berkeley Digby George Sheffield, the eldest son of the 5th Baronet, Robert Sheffield, who was born in London. This picture was taken by Winterton photographer James Walsham Hall.

Construction of the new Servants' Wing is in progress in this view of the Hall in 1906. It was part of the extensions designed by the architect, Walter Brierley.

The rear of the east side of the new Servants' Wing in 1907. It replaced a smaller wing on the same site, but lasted only four decades before it was demolished in 1949.

The Hall from the south, across the new sunken garden, which was also part of the new extensions. Walter Brierley's East Wing can be seen on the right.

Leonard Newell, the Normanby Hall butler, took this snapshot of the dining room laid out for a meal, in around 1937. It is now the Hall's banqueting room.

Planting a tulip tree in the Park on 26 October 1933, to commemorate the visit of HM King George V's fourth son, HRH Prince George, the Duke of Kent. Opposite him is Sir Berkeley Sheffield, with Mr P. Stanworth, the Head Woodman, holding the tree. This was the day of the Prince's official visit to Scunthorpe, when he stayed overnight at the Hall.

Normanby Hall staff, taken in the grounds of the Hall in 1926. Sitting on the donkey is Hilda Brunt, who worked in the kitchen, with one of the footmen in uniform standing next to her. The donkey was used each day to move household rubbish from the Hall.

Loch Morar on the west coast of Scotland in the 1920s. Members of the Normanby Hall domestic staff are in the launch, on their way to the Sheffield family shooting lodge at Meoble Forrest. The family regularly stayed here for the grouse shooting season in August. The snapshot was taken by Hilda Brunt.

Domestic staff in the sunken garden in 1937, when the family were resident in London for the 'Season'. Clockwise from the left are Mrs Drayton (cleaner), Miss Richardson (sewing help), Dora Dickens (housemaid) and Lena Ripley (housemaid).

The main drive leading to the Park entrance opposite Normanby village, c. 1915. A hidden 'servants' walk' ran alongside it on the right. Servants were not allowed to walk up the main drive.

Kennel-maid Maggie Dent on one of the horses in the stableyard at Normanby in the 1920s. She was the daughter of Jack Dent, the Head Gamekeeper, and looked after a number of dogs in the Park, which were mainly used for shooting.

This 48 horse power dark blue Daimler was one of the first motorcars at Normanby Hall. It was taken in the stableyard after 1912, when the Coach House range was converted into garages.

Outside the tea tent at the annual Normanby Estates Agricultural & Horticultural Show, held on 25 July 1907. The show began in 1884 and soon became one of the highlights of the year in the Normanby area, as well as attracting visitors from further afield. There were competitions for livestock, poultry, flowers and vegetables, bands, sporting events and amusements, not least of which was the chance to enjoy the gardens and greenhouses in the Park. The show was suspended at the outbreak of the First World War and never recommenced.

The flower marquee at the 1907 show.

Normanby village in 1906, looking towards Burton-upon-Stather. At this time all the cottages were owned by the Sheffield family, and many were allocated to their estate staff. Most people could afford bicycles by this time and the lady on the right, and two of the children, are showing off their new machines.

The Normanby Estate Clerk of Works' house at the east end of Normanby village was built in 1893. Lucy Beacock, the daughter of Charles Beacock, the Clerk of Works, is standing at the front gate in this photograph, taken in 1938.

Interior of the joiner's shop in the Estate Yard in 1907. The Estate Yard consisted of various different workshops and stores, and was the service centre of the Normanby Estate.

The Estate Yard also had a power house, which generated electricity for the Hall, including the Servants' Wing, where the staff enjoyed the benefits of central heating and electric lighting. It is seen here in 1907.

Head Gamekeeper Jack Dent with Labrador dogs on Crosby Warren between the wars.

During the First World War, Normanby Hall was used as a Voluntary Aid Detachment Hospital for convalescing soldiers, some of whom can be seen here on the steps outside the front entrance. It was attached to the 3rd Northern General Hospital in Sheffield, and all of the ground floor was turned into a hospital. The Commandant was Lady Julia Sheffield, who was praised for personally nursing the recuperating servicemen. She is wearing the black cap in the back row.

This is Louise Denton ARRC, the Sister-Charge of Normanby Hall throughout the First World War.

Recuperating soldiers sitting outside Normanby Hall during a fancy dress party to celebrate the end of the First World War.

11
WINTERTON

Winterton Market Place at the centre of the town. Churchside, leading to All Saints' parish church, is in the background, and the shop on the right is the local branch of the Scunthorpe Co-operative Society, opened in 1914. The third building on the right is the George Hotel, a former coaching house dating from the eighteenth century.

Winterton High Street in 1916, looking towards the Market Place. The inn sign of the Butchers' Arms public house can be seen on the right.

The official opening of Winterton All Saints' Church Institute in the High Street in 1903.

King Street before the First World War, with Blankney House in the background. Opposite the Cross Keys Hotel is George Waterlow's shop, who was a bicycle and early motorcar dealer.

Winterton Gas Company supplied the gas for lamps like the one on the left of this photograph in King Street, seen here in around 1910.

Winterton Wesleyan Methodist Chapel on the south side of King Street. This was the third in the town, opened on 20 March 1878 by the Revd J.B. Pope, at a cost of £3,000. A lecture hall was added in 1892, and it was replaced by the present-day Methodist Chapel on the same site in 1962.

Park Street looking east in 1930, at the junction with Hart Lane, where King Street joins Park Street.

Most of the houses are still standing today in this view looking along Northlands Road towards the junction with West Street.

This distinctive house at 53 West Street is known as The Chains and was the home of Winterton's most famous son, the architect, engraver and furniture designer William Fowler (1761-1832). It dates from the late eighteenth century and was probably rebuilt by him in a mixture of Tudor and early Gothic Revival style. He became nationally known for his engravings of Roman mosaic pavements and stained glass, and was presented to Queen Charlotte at Windsor Castle in 1814. His son, Joseph Fowler, also an architect and builder, lived here after his marriage in 1828.

Above: All Saints' parish church, viewed from the east. The earliest parts of the church date from the twelfth century, but it is mainly built in the Early English style in limestone. It was restored in 1867 and 1903.

Left: The interior of All Saints', looking east towards the chancel.

North Street from the south in the 1950s.

Another view further along North Street in the 1950s. The agricultural engineering firm of T. & J. Fletcher have traded at their Newport Ironworks in North Street for over 150 years, and are still operating there today.

Queen Street looking north after 1900. George Harrison's off-license is on the corner of Chapel Lane on the right. He was an agent for the Tadcaster Tower Brewery Company. The Primitive Methodist Chapel on the left was opened on the site of a previous chapel in 1879, and could seat 550 worshippers.

Decorated bicycles outside Edwin Willford's draper and grocers shop in King Street, during the Winterton celebrations for the Diamond Jubilee of Queen Victoria in 1897.

The Old Hall in Park Street, *c.* 1930. It dated back to the seventeenth century, and is thought to have been built on the site of a Medieval manor house. It was the home of the Stovin family, but this fine house was unfortunately demolished in 1973.

A garden party in the grounds of Winterton Hall on West Street, given by William Sawyer in August 1910. The Hall was built in the Classical style by William Marris in the late eighteenth century

A *carte-de-visite* portrait of James Walsham Hall (1819-1902). He was the eldest of William and Elizabeth Hall's twelve children, and spent most of his life in Winterton, where he was first a joiner, then a grocer in North Street. However, he is much better known as a semi-professional photographer working between the 1860s and 1890s; the first in Scunthorpe and district. As well as many studio portraits, he also took views of Winterton, nearby villages, and the first photographs of the new ironworks in Scunthorpe.

Market Street taken by Walsham Hall, probably in 1872, when the garlands would have been celebrating the restoration of All Saints' Church. He chose a time when all the shops were closed, including the long-standing Tate family watchmaker's, jeweller's and ironmonger's shop on the right.

A Walsham Hall photograph of cottages on the south side of King Street, also probably taken in 1872.

Prizes laid out in front of a grandstand at Winterton Agricultural Society's Annual Show on 3 July 1909. It began in 1872 and was always known as the 'Midsummer Show'.

Cycle racing has been a part of the Winterton Show since the 1880s and is one of the oldest grass track meetings in the country. Its popularity is shown by the large crowds at the start of a race in this Edwardian photograph. It was the scene of many titanic battles in the 1920s and '30s involving Albert 'Lal' White, a national cycling champion from Scunthorpe.

Members of Winterton Rangers FC during their first season after the First World War.

An early morning start to a charabanc outing in the 1920s, outside Scunthorpe Co-operative Society's Winterton branch in the Market Place.

Other titles published by The History Press

Doncaster: Through the Lens of Luke Bagshaw
PETER TUFFREY

Each of these images is accompanied by a detailed caption. Some are extremely rare, including shots of Doncaster colliery at the turn of the century and the inside of the railway works of the Victorian age. With events such as the Chrysanthemum Show and a tea party at Cusworth Hall, busy street scenes, views of the surrounding area and the full history of Doncaster's Victorian buildings, theatres and pubs – as well as long-gone institutions such as the workhouse – this volume will delight photographers and local historians alike.

978 0 7524 4807 7

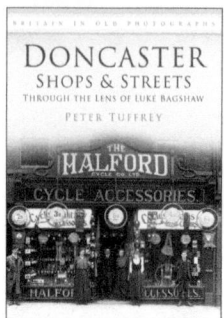

Doncaster Shops & Streets: Through the Lens of Luke Bagshaw
PETER TUFFREY

This fascinating collection, taken from the original glass-plate negatives, showcases some of the very best of local photographer Luke Bagshaw's images of Doncaster at the turn of the last century. Balby Laundry, E.H. Booth's grocers, Bell Brother's jewellers, W.E. Clark's cycle shop and countless others are all captured in Bagshaw's beautiful images.

978 0 7524 4837 4

Hanged at Leeds
STEVE FIELDING

For decades the high walls of Leeds' Armley Gaol have contained many infamous criminals. Men and women who paid the ultimate penalty here include notorious cat burglar and killer Charles Peace; Emily Swann and her lover John Gallagher, hanged together for the murder of her husband; two young army deserters executed for the brutal slaying of a Pontefract shopkeeper; along with gangland thugs from Sheffield, spurned lovers, cut-throat murderers and many more.

978 0 7509 5093 0

Who's There? The True Story of a Leeds Haunting
COLETTE SHIRES

'Then, adding horror to horror, a pair of thin, long-fingered hands placed themselves on my stomach and proceeded to inch their way up my body. They crawled underneath my own hands resting on my chest ... As they neared my throat, I thought I was about to die.' When the Shires family heard what sounded like a baby crying in their new house, they had no idea that it was the beginning of a terrifying haunting that would last for more than thirty years, and follow them across the city. This is their story.

978 0 7524 4808 4

Visit our website and discover thousands of other History Press books.

www.thehistorypress.co.uk